THE BEST OF
COLLEGE
Basketball

by Gregory N. Peters

CAPSTONE PRESS
a capstone imprint

Trailblazers Books are published by Capstone Press,
1710 Roe Crest Drive, North Mankato, Minnesota 56003
www.capstonepub.com

Library of Congress Cataloging-in-Publication Data
Peters, Gregory N.
The best of college basketball / by Gregory N. Peters.
pages cm. — (Trailblazers. sports and recreation)
Includes bibliographical references and index.
Summary: "Describes the NCAA College Basketball Tournament, including
teams, players, and coaches"—Provided by publisher.
ISBN 978-1-4765-8521-5 (library binding)
1. NCAA Basketball Tournament—Juvenile literature. I. Title
GV885.49.N37P48 2014
 796.323'63—dc23   2013030187

Editorial Credits

Christine Peterson, editor; Gene Bentdahl, designer; Eric Gohl, media
researcher; Eric Manske, production specialist

Photo Credits

AP Photo: 19, 42, Bob Jordan, 26, Carlos Osorio, 38, Chris Steppig/NCAA
Photos, cover; Corbis: Bettmann, 16, 21, 29, 32, Wally McNamee, 18, ZUMA
Press/Kevin Sullivan, 31; Getty Images: Focus on Sport, 22, Jonathan Daniel,
25; Newscom: Cal Sport Media/Bill Shettle, 36, Icon SMI/AJ Mast, 15, Icon
SMI/Chris Pondy, 12, Icon SMI/Robin Alam, 8, MCT/Charles Bertram, 9, MCT/
Harry E. Walker, 11, MCT/Mark Cornelison, 34, MCT/Rich Sugg, 4, ZUMA
Press/Brian Spurlock, 40; Shutterstock: SAJE, 7

Printed in China by Nordica.
1013/CA21301911
029013   007739NORDS14

TABLE OF CONTENTS

CHAPTER 1

The Tournament

The NCAA Men's Division I Basketball Championship

The score is 78-77. There are three seconds left on the clock. One basket will win the game. The crowd is going crazy. The players' hearts are racing. The ball is dribbled down the court. Three, two, one, the shot is up. It's good!

Have you heard the name Magic Johnson or Christian Laettner? What about big-time coaches? Do you know Dean Smith, Jimmy Valvano, or Coach K? All of these people are part of college basketball history.

In March the NCAA (National **Collegiate** Athletic Association) has its men's basketball **championship**. This **tournament** decides the best college basketball team in the country.

---

collegiate – related to a college

championship – the final game of the NCAA tournament

tournament – a contest in which the winner is the one who wins the most games

---

The tournament starts in March. Each year, about 350 teams compete for a chance to play in the tournament. In the end, only 68 teams make it. The teams work hard all year to be in this **elite** group. Picked teams compete in "The Big Dance." This is not on a dance floor. It is on a basketball court. Instead of dancing, there's dribbling, shooting, and running.

The NCAA **committee** watches games all year. Committee members choose the 68 teams. They pick the teams on the Sunday before the tournament starts. The chosen teams are seeded from 1 to 16.

The number 1 seeds are the teams that the committee thinks are the best. Once the teams are seeded, they are put into one of four groups called brackets. The bracket depends on what **geographical** region the team represents. In 2012 the regions were called South, East, Midwest, and West.

elite – a group of people considered to be the best

committee – a group of people chosen to discuss things and make decisions for a larger group

geographical – relating to geography

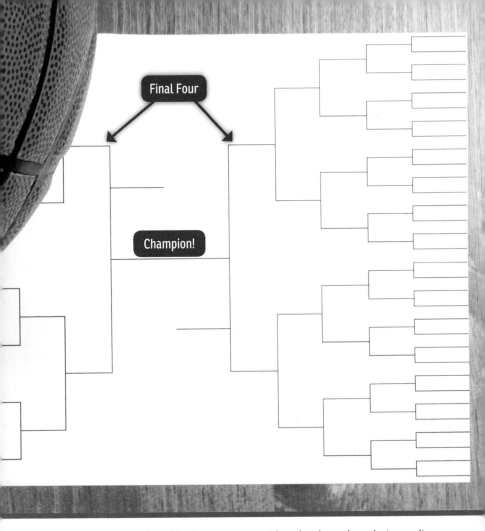

Final Four

Champion!

Teams are placed in the tournament bracket based on their seeding.

Some schools usually have good teams. Their teams often play in the tournament. Some teams are new to the tournament. They are excited for the chance to compete.

Women's college teams also compete in a March tournament. They have the same rules. They have seeds and brackets too.

The Final Four

When the tournament starts, teams are ready to play. The first round starts in mid-March. There are many games. The teams that lose go home. The teams that win play another team that has won. Soon there are only 16 teams left. They are called the Sweet Sixteen.

The Sweet Sixteen teams play each other. When those games are done, there are eight teams left. These teams are called the Elite Eight. Those eight teams then play each other. The winning teams are part of the Final Four.

Teams that make it to the Final Four are playing at the top of their game. They beat many teams. It takes a lot of hard work to reach this level.

Players celebrate a victory during the NCAA tournament in 2012.

Perfect Seasons

Some teams have won every game. UCLA has had four perfect seasons. They were in 1964, 1967, 1972, and 1973.

The Championship Game

The Final Four teams play each other. Only two teams are left. That means it's time for the championship game. Fans come from all over the country to watch the game. Millions of others watch on TV. The winner gets the NCAA college basketball title and is the best college team that year.

Many teams have been champions. The University of California, Los Angeles (UCLA) has won 11 times. That's a record. The University of Kentucky's team has the next most wins with eight.

There is a special **tradition** at the end of the championship game. The winning team cuts down the basketball net. This tradition started in the late 1940s. The coach that year wanted a **souvenir** of the game. Fans stay when the game is over. They want to watch this special moment.

Final Four Bound
The University of North Carolina Tar Heels have made it to the Final Four a record 18 times!

tradition - a custom, idea, or belief passed down through time

souvenir - something that is a reminder of a special event

Anthony Davis of the Kentucky Wildcats cuts down the net after the 2012 NCAA tournament.

Russ Smith of the Louisville Cardinals looks for an open teammate during the 2012 tournament.

CHAPTER 2

Hoop Legends

Why do people play basketball? Because it's fun. Basketball is a great sport. Almost anyone can play. You don't have to be tall or strong. You can play with your friends. It's also fun to be a fan. There have been many great players to cheer for.

Center of Attention

There are five players on the court for each team. The center on a basketball team is usually the tallest player. Being tall makes some things easier for the center. They try to get close to the basket to score. They try to block shots and grab the ball if someone misses a shot. They also guard the other team's center. Many have the nickname "big man." The center's role is very important.

Cody Zeller from Indiana University pulls in a rebound.

Lew Alcindor

Lew Alcindor was a famous center. He played for UCLA's basketball team. He's a very tall man. He is 7 feet 2 inches (218 centimeters). He joined the UCLA team in 1965. While he was on the team, UCLA won three NCAA championships.

Bill Walton

Another famous UCLA center was Bill Walton. While he was playing, the team won 88 games in a row.

Alcindor was also a good student. He graduated with a history degree. His teammates and classmates said he is a gentle and kind man.

Alcindor's best shot was called the "sky-hook." It was easy for him because he was so tall. He could **dunk** too. He could put the ball right in the basket. In 1967 the rules changed. Dunking wasn't allowed. Eleven years later players could dunk again. Many players in the NCAA dunk today.

After college Alcindor played in the National Basketball Association (NBA). He did very well. He scored 38,387 points in his career. That's more points than anyone else ever scored. He also grabbed many rebounds and blocked many shots. He was one of the best centers of all time.

Maybe you have never heard of Lew Alcindor. That might be because he changed his name in 1971. While he was in college, he became a **Muslim**, which means he followed the religion of Islam. He changed his name. Lew Alcindor became Kareem Abdul-Jabbar.

dunk – when a player jumps and puts the ball directly through the hoop

Muslim – someone who follows the religion of Islam

17

Georgetown University also had a great center on its team. Patrick Ewing played for Georgetown in the 1980s. He was 7 feet (213 cm) tall. He was one of the best players of that time. He took his team to the Final Four three times. He was not just a great player. Ewing promised his mom he would stay in college until he got his degree. He kept his promise.

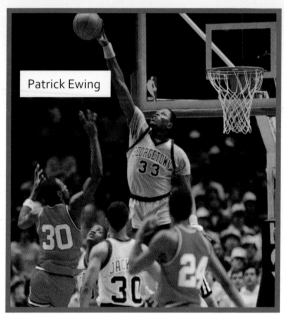

Patrick Ewing

Triple Threats

Some players are good at many positions. They can play all over the court. These players are called "triple threats." They can score, **rebound**, and **assist**. These are three things that help teams win. Scoring means getting the ball in the basket. Rebounding is just as important. When a player misses a shot, everyone tries to grab the ball. If you get the ball for your team, you get a rebound. An assist is when a player passes a ball to a teammate who scores.

Oscar Robertson

Oscar Robertson was a great guard. His main job was to dribble and pass the basketball. But Robertson was also a triple threat. He was known as "The Big O."

rebound – the act of gaining control of the ball after a missed shot

assist – a pass that leads to a score by a teammate

Robertson played college basketball in the late 1950s. He played for the University of Cincinnati. **Racism** was common at that time. His white teammates could stay in hotels when the team traveled. Robertson had to stay in college **dorms**. Many hotels didn't allow African-Americans.

Robertson couldn't be stopped on the court. He averaged 33.8 points per game. He also averaged 15.2 rebounds per game. His team went to the Final Four twice. In one of the games, he had 39 points. He also had 17 rebounds and 10 assists. The NCAA Player of the Year Trophy is named after him. Robertson also co-captained the 1960 **Olympic** Men's Basketball team. The Olympics is a worldwide sports competition. The team won a gold medal. Robertson went on to play basketball in the NBA.

racism – the belief that one race is better than others

dorm – a place where students live in college

Olympics – a competition of many sports events held every four years in a different country; people from around the world compete against each other

Magic Johnson drives to the hoop during a 1979 NCAA game.

    Magic Johnson is another famous triple threat. His real first name is Earvin. He got his nickname from a writer. When he saw Earvin play he called it "magic." The name stuck. Johnson played for Michigan State University in East Lansing. In one big game in college, he scored 29 points. He also had 10 rebounds and 10 assists. Later he played in the NBA for the Los Angeles Lakers.

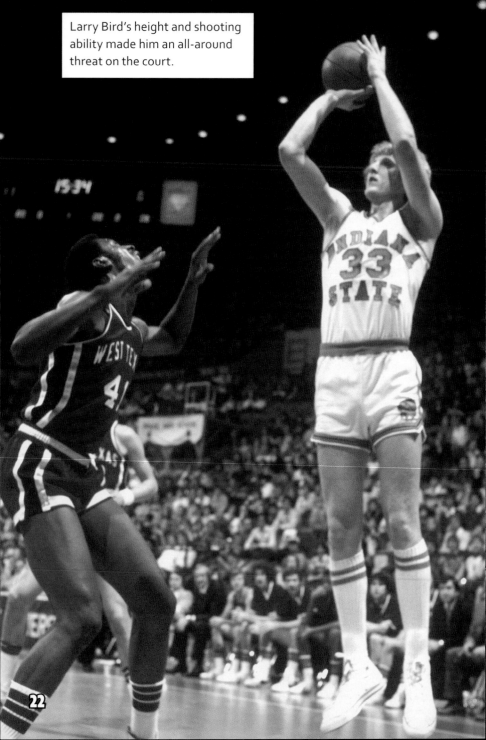

Larry Bird's height and shooting ability made him an all-around threat on the court.

Forward Thinking

Each basketball team has five players on the court. Usually, there is one center, two guards, and two forwards. A forward usually tries to pass and take outside shots. They also rebound and try to stop the other team from scoring.

Larry Bird was one of the best forwards ever. Bird grew up in the state of Indiana. He played at Indiana State University. It was a small school near his home. Bird became an All-American. He became one of the top players in the country. His school was small, but his team was great.

In 1979 his team played Magic Johnson's team for the NCAA championship. It was thrilling. Two of the best players were on the court. Millions of people watched the game. Bird's team lost. The final score was 75-64.

Even though he lost, he went on to a great career. He moved to Boston, Massachusetts. There he played for the Boston Celtics in the NBA. He was a superstar for many years. Bird and Johnson played against each other many times in the NBA.

Some forwards are called power forwards. They are big players who can also play center. One of the best was Christian Laettner. He played for Duke University from 1988 to 1992. While he was there they won the championship twice. They made it to the Final Four an amazing four times. He has said two things helped him play his best: getting rest and eating well. Being almost 7 feet (213 cm) tall does not hurt either! Laettner left Duke in 1992. He went to the NBA and played on five different teams.

Christian Laettner (32) puts up a shot over a defender.

Dean Smith

CHAPTER 3

The Coaches

What makes a great team? Having great players is important. But it's the coaches who hold the team together. They help the players get better.

Dean Smith

Dean Smith was the coach at the University of North Carolina. He was the coach there for 36 years. His teams won two NCAA titles. They played in the Final Four 11 times. Smith is a coaching **legend** and a caring man. He brought Charlie Scott to his school. Scott was the school's first African-American player. Smith's players were very good. They were also smart. Coach Smith made sure they studied hard. Ninety-six percent of his players stayed in college until they got their degrees. That's a winning record.

> **legend** - a person who is famous for accomplishing great things

John Wooden

Coach John Wooden was a man with strong **beliefs**. He worked hard with his players. He wanted them to be good at basketball. He also wanted them to be good people. In 1948 Wooden became the coach at UCLA. His teams were the best. They won the NCAA championship 10 times. They won every year from 1967 to 1973. That's seven championships in a row. For a long while, it seemed they couldn't lose. His team once won 88 games without losing. Wooden was named national coach of the year six times.

Coach Wooden died in 2010. He was 99 years old. Every year two **outstanding** college basketball players get the John R. Wooden Trophy. One is a male player, and one is a female player. The trophy is in honor of this truly great coach.

John Wooden challenged and encouraged his players.

belief – something you think is true or correct

outstanding – exceptionally good

Mike Krzyzewski

Mike Krzyzewski (pronounced sha-SHEF-ski) is known as "Coach K." He has been the coach of Duke's basketball team since 1980. The Duke Blue Devils are one of the best teams in college basketball. The Blue Devils have four NCAA titles. They have been in the Final Four 15 times. Coach K was their coach each time they won a championship.

Beating Knight's Record

Coach K was a basketball player at Indiana University when he was young. His coach in college was Bob Knight. Knight became his friend. Knight had won a record 902 games. In 2011 Coach K beat Knight's record. He is still coaching and winning.

Krzyzewski was the head coach for the USA men's basketball team at the 2008 and 2012 Olympics. Team USA brought home the gold both years.

Coach Valvano celebrates with his players after N.C. State upset Houston in the championship game.

CHAPTER 4

Surprise Teams

There are teams that no one thinks will make it far in the NCAA tournament. They end up surprising everyone. It shows people that hard work pays off.

In 1983 Jimmy Valvano coached North Carolina State University. His team was a low seed. They were not expected to win. But they kept winning close games. They surprised a lot of people. They reached the finals. The biggest surprise was still to come.

The last game was close. With seconds remaining the score was tied. Either team could win. One of Valvano's players took a shot. He missed. His teammate Lorenzo Charles grabbed the ball. Charles jumped up and dunked it. The game was over. N.C. State had won! Valvano ran around the court. He was so excited. He wanted to hug everyone.

Butler's Gordon Hayward puts up a shot in the last 10 seconds of the 2010 championship. Hayward's shot missed, and Butler lost to Duke 61-59.

In 1985 another school surprised people. The Villanova Wildcats were ranked eighth in their region. That did not matter to them. They played Georgetown in the championship game. Georgetown was a number 1 seed. Almost no one expected Villanova to beat mighty Georgetown. It was a close game. The final score was 64-62. Villanova had won! It was a happy surprise for Villanova fans.

A more recent surprise story is Butler University. Butler is a small college. It has only about 5,000 students. Small schools don't usually beat big schools. Bigger schools have more money. They can **recruit** better players. That means they have a better chance of getting players to come to their schools. But during the NCAA tournament anything can happen. Teams can play surprisingly well and come out on top.

In 2010 Butler was the fifth-seeded team. They were not expected to win. But they played hard and made it to the championship game. It happened again the next year. This time they were the eighth-seeded team. Again they made it to the championship game. Butler has reached the Final Four three times. It's a small college that delivers big surprises.

recruit - to ask someone to join a college team

Baylor defeated Notre Dame in 2012 to win the women's NCAA championship.

CHAPTER 5

Record Setters

Sometimes players save their best for the tournament. They are excited and have a lot of energy. They know the games are a big deal. If they lose, they are done. They have to win to keep playing. They also know if they do well it means a lot for their future. They have a better chance to play professionally. For many college players, that would be a dream come true.

Ty Lawson

Austin Carr played for the University of Notre Dame's team. Carr wasn't a big player. But he was strong and quick. In 1970 Carr was in a tournament game against Ohio University. He was playing great. He was scoring lots of points. His coach wanted to take him out of the game. He thought Carr needed a rest. Good thing he changed his mind. Carr scored a record-breaking 61 points that day. No one has broken that record since.

Ty Lawson is a basketball thief. He is a master at taking the ball away from the other team. Lawson played for the North Carolina Tar Heels. In 2009 he stole the ball eight times in the championship game. That's a record. Lawson was the top player in that game in other ways too. He also scored 21 points. His team won by 17 points.

Shaquille O'Neal (33) gets in position to block a shot.

Shaquille O'Neal is an all-time great player. As a professional basketball player, he played for the Orlando Magic and the Los Angeles Lakers. He became known as "Shaq." In college he played for Louisiana State University. In 1992 his college team was playing Brigham Young University from Provo, Utah. In that game Shaq blocked 11 shots. No one has broken this record since.

What about rebounds? Fred Cohen of Temple University holds that record. He had 34 rebounds in a single game in 1956. A few people have come close to this record. But no one has beaten him yet.

Fewest Points

Records are not always good things. St. Louis University holds the record for the fewest points scored in a game. On January 10, 2008, the St. Louis team scored only 20 points in a game.

Pistol Pete

Pete Maravich and his Louisiana State team never got close to a national title. But "Pistol Pete" was one of the most exciting college players ever. Maravich scored a record 3,667 points. That's an average of 44.2 points per game.

NCAA Records

Top three winning colleges of all time:

- UCLA: 11
- Kentucky: 8
- Indiana: 5

Coaches with most tournament wins:

- Mike Krzyzewski (Duke): 77
- Dean Smith (North Carolina): 65
- Roy Williams (Kansas, North Carolina): 50
- John Wooden (UCLA): 47

Coaches with most Final Four appearances:

- John Wooden: 12
- Dean Smith: 11
- Mike Krzyzewski: 11
- Roy Williams: 7

Amazing facts:

- Pistol Pete's coach was his father, Press Maravich.
- Pistol did not play in his first year in college. Freshmen were not allowed to play then. If he had played, he probably would have scored many more points.
- There was no three-point line when Maravich played. Many of Pete's shots were from far away. Those baskets counted as only two points.

Read More

Bekkering, Annalise. *NCAA Basketball.* Pro Sports Championships. New York: AV² by Weigl, 2013.

Doeden, Matt. *The Best of Pro Basketball.* Best of Pro Sports. Mankato, Minn.: Capstone Press, 2010.

Hurley, Michael. *Basketball.* Fantastic Sports Facts. Chicago: Capstone Raintree, 2013.

Rich, Francine Poppo. *Larry Bird: The Boy from French Lick.* West Bay Shore, N.Y.: Blue Marlin Publications, 2009.

Schulte, Mary E. *The Final Four: All about College Basketball's Biggest Event.* Winner Takes All. Mankato, Minn.: Capstone Press, 2013.

Silverman, Drew. *Basketball.* Best Sport Ever. Minneapolis: ABDO Pub. Co., 2012.

Woods, Mark, and Ruth Owen. *Slam Dunk!: Basketball Facts and Stats.* Top Score Math. New York: Gareth Stevens, 2011.

Internet Sites

FactHound offers a safe, fun way to find Internet sites related to this book. All of the sites on FactHound have been researched by our staff.

Here's all you do:
Visit *www.facthound.com*
Type in this code: 9781476585215

 Check out projects, games and lots more at
www.capstonekids.com

Titles in this set:

The Best of College Basketball

Muhammad Ali Boxing Legend

The Negro Leagues

Serena and Venus Williams Tennis Stars

Glossary

assist (uh-SIST) • a pass that leads to a score by a teammate

belief (buh-LEEF) • something you think is true or correct

championship (CHAM-pee-uhn-ship) • the final game of the NCAA tournament

collegiate (kuh-LEE-jit) • related to a college

committee (kuh-MI-tee) • a group of people chosen to discuss things and make decisions for a larger group

dorm (DOHRM) • a place where students live in college

dunk (DUNK) • when a player jumps and puts the ball directly through the hoop

elite (ih-LEET) • a group of people considered to be the best

geographical (jee-uh-GRAF-i-kuhl) • relating to geography

legend (LEJ-uhnd) • a person who is famous for accomplishing great things

Muslim (MUHZ-luhm) • someone who follows the religion of Islam

Olympics (oh-LIM-piks) • a competition of many sports events held every four years in a different country; people from around the world compete against each other

outstanding (out-STAN-ding) • exceptionally good

racism (RAY-siz-uhm) • the belief that one race is better than others

rebound (REE-bound) • the act of gaining control of the ball after a missed shot

recruit (ri-KROOT) • to ask someone to join a college team

souvenir (SOO-vuh-neer) • something that is a reminder of a special event

tournament (TUR-nuh-muhnt) • a contest in which the winner is the one who wins the most games

tradition (truh-DISH-uhn) • a custom, idea, or belief passed down through time

Index